THE
WELL-LOVED
HOUSE

THE WELL-LOVED HOUSE

CREATING HOMES WITH COLOR, COMFORT, AND DRAMA

ASHLEY WHITTAKER

FOREWORD BY CHRISTOPHER SPITZMILLER

PRINCIPAL PHOTOGRAPHY BY THOMAS LOOF

RIZZOLI
NEW YORK

New York · Paris · London · Milan

To my mother, Barbara Whittaker,
for teaching me early on the importance of
truly living in and loving your house.

CONTENTS

FOREWORD

Comfortable, classic American style is what comes to mind when I think of Ashley Whittaker's interiors. It's the kind of comfort that Sister Parish so often showed her clients when she took them to an upholstery workroom and famously lay down on a sofa to demonstrate how the piece was intended to be enjoyed. Ashley's rooms embody this kind of relaxed ease, the all-too-elusive livable comfort, while remaining classic and refined.

When I walk into one of her interiors, I am enveloped by a feeling of warmth thanks to the color of the walls, the mix of patterns, and the various materials she uses. This feeling of coziness comes from more than just the upholstery, of course—it is established through an expert layering of the entire room as a complete cohesive composition.

Ashley's approach to creating beautiful spaces for her clients starts with her attuned ability to listen and discover what type of house they want to call home. She then intuitively and effortlessly starts her work to realize that vision. Interior design is a process that takes one down a road not always easy to travel, but Ashley never makes it feel difficult (for herself or her clients).

I am friends with more than a few decorators, but none are as close friends as Ashley. We laugh together at our trials and tribulations and share our triumphs and joys. When we make plans, we always see them through; there is no canceling or rescheduling for us. To have someone like her in my life, who treats me more like a brother than a friend, is a rare gift—much like the comfort and style she imparts to her very fortunate clients.   —*Christopher Spitzmiller*

INTRODUCTION

My earliest memories of home are of a bright, sunny house, well loved and well used, memories that inspire the way I approach design today. My mother, who has innately beautiful taste, worked with a good friend who was a decorator to create pretty, light-filled rooms, cheerful but not overdone. The heart of our house—the room in which we lived as a family and where my mother entertained—was a vaulted, double-height space with French doors opening to the pool. My mother called it the Florida room—a throwback to her childhood in Greenwich, Connecticut, I know, but a name that always made me laugh since we already lived in Florida. The elements changed as they needed to, but there was never a major reinvention. When the curtains were faded from the sun, new ones were ordered. When one too many Bloody Marys were spilled on the rug—it was the '70s, after all—we replaced it. This taught me to see decoration as an evolution and to value spaces that feel collected over time. For my bedroom, my mother selected beautiful sheets and coverlets, organized pretty bookshelves, and hung nice paintings. I remember pining for the fun of my friends' rooms, with brightly hued bedding and walls covered in posters. In retrospect, mine gave me an appreciation for beautiful things and for the comfort and pleasure a finished space offers.

My mother sold real estate when I was growing up, and I spent much of my childhood in Florida tagging along with her to open houses. She still laughs about ten-year-old me pronouncing: "You know, if there were French doors in the dining room leading to the terrace, there would be much more light in here." In those days, I used to devour my mother's issues of *House & Garden*, *House Beautiful*, and *Architectural Digest* that arrived like clockwork each month. Like the best textbooks, they taught me to admire all the greats: Albert Hadley, Sister Parish, Mario Buatta, David Easton, and so many others. I saved pages from those magazines for future projects, even though I did not quite know what the future would bring.

College was the first time I took the plunge into decorating for myself. When I arrived at my ramshackle, off-campus house, I discovered that my bedroom was painted red—and I just couldn't bear it. I remembered I had a few rolls of unused Laura Ashley wallpaper at home. I carried them back with me after Thanksgiving vacation, marched to the local hardware store, got a staple gun, and went to town covering my bedroom walls. This was my first foray into decorating. And after dangling off a ladder with a staple gun for three days, safe to say it was my last for many years.

For nine years after college, I worked in the public relations department at Ralph Lauren, planning PR campaigns as well as large events and fashion shows. Ralph made everything he did thrilling, special, and beautiful. Immersion in the world he created—living and breathing it to the last detail day after day— taught me to really see. Eventually I left to try corporate event planning at Forstmann, Little & Co., but I soon realized I would much rather spend an afternoon with legendary event planner Robert Isabell in his studio designing the event than poring over guest lists and seating charts in a conference room on the forty-fourth floor. This is when I knew I needed to change direction and put my creativity to work for myself. I called my friend, decorator Markham Roberts. Two years in his office taught me much about the keys to making houses comfortable and appealing, about how necessary it is to have a clear knowledge of the history of design and a vision for how each room will live.

Since founding my own firm in 2007, I have had such wonderful opportunities to explore all different types of solutions in locations ranging from the beach to the mountains and from the country to the city. Each client has his or her own idea of a dream home and family lifestyle. Every project teaches me that much more about the best way to make those visions real, whether it involves renovating a historic or contemporary house or collaborating on a home from conception to completion.

When I was fortunate enough to be able to create my own house from the ground up, my life came full circle in a way. I put everything I had learned about what makes a house feel well loved and complete to work. For my family and the way we live, I balanced the importance of practicality with the necessity of beauty to the last detail.

Everything I do as a designer stems from the love of home. Decoration is just the tool I use for expressing this love in tangible terms. That said, if the sofa arms are not worn through and the rugs are still pristine after ten years, then I have not done my job. But when the rooms show the marks of family life over time, I know I have achieved my goal: a house lived in and well loved.

TWENTY-FIRST CENTURY TRADITIONAL

I believe that decoration is a way to celebrate life, including its rites of passage, like leaving Manhattan for the suburbs as a family grows. So when this young couple, longtime New York clients, welcomed their fifth son, purchasing this 1920s stone house in Greenwich, Connecticut, made perfect sense. The house flowed beautifully for their active family life and frequent entertaining. Architect George Knight had recently brought it back to its former glory. Plus, its gracious, expansive interiors still sang with much of the original architectural detail.

The living room, light-filled and open, had happily retained the salon-like dimensions of its original era. But I wanted to make it as comfortable for two to read quietly by the fire as for fifty to gather for cocktails, so I worked some classic planning magic—divide, conquer, repeat—using twin rugs to anchor separate seating areas connected by substantial matching sofas.

OPPOSITE: This Gracie paper emphasizes the scale of the double-height entry hall and lays the foundation for the color palette throughout. The sconces help the eye to travel, creating an inviting connection between the floors. The space under the stairs is transformed into a destination with the addition of a Georgian settee.

I love the history of decorating, and I often turn to the legends for inspiration—and so does my client. Through all of our work together, we have always returned to an Albert Hadley room from the 1970s with peacock-blue lacquered walls and a chevron-patterned stained floor as an ideal of perfection. In the dining room, with its gorgeous original paneling still intact after almost a century, we both felt we had finally found the perfect spot to create our version of this iconic room.

The library still had its original oak paneling, but an awkward floor plan. We decided to address this by eliminating one of the two doors to the hallway. This created a nook just right for a nine-foot sofa. The finishing touch was waxing the paneled walls to a soft glow, bringing the room to life.

There was a neglected pass-through between the entrance hall and the kitchen. Because of its proximity to the kitchen, it had the potential to become a great space for morning coffee as well as a children's hangout. To bring this idea to life—and in the spirit of reduce, reuse, recycle—I installed one of the floor-to-ceiling Russian-style cabinets from the clients' last apartment (just right for stowing board games) and designed a banquette for lounging.

The bedrooms upstairs needed their own unique decorating calculus. In the principal bedroom, I mounted a half tester over the bed, which creates a sense of a room within a room. The boys' bedrooms were all about playfulness and fun, with patterns and palettes that could grow with them. In other words, the decoration was a celebration of life in the moment—and as it moves forward.

OPPOSITE: The hall table is from a Kips Bay Show House room designed by Charlotte Moss; we found it at auction and revitalized it with a new peacock-blue leather top. The basket does double duty, adding storage and filling the volume. OVERLEAF: The photograph by Carol Bouyoucos relaxes this otherwise formal room, organically bringing in a modern note. The rug walks the line between graphic and elegant.

OPPOSITE: Sometimes the view into the rooms beyond—the scenic paper of the hall and the bright blue lacquer of the dining room—is as important as the room itself. ABOVE, CLOCKWISE FROM TOP LEFT: Plants and flowers bring a room to life; an embroidered tape trim adds definition to these ivory wool curtains; Quadrille pillows from the family's previous home are part of the evolving story; the chair's blue silk ikat participates in the room's pattern play.

Decorating is all about relationships. My goal for each room—and the entire house—is to find just the right mix that serves the purpose.

CONTRAST

Every house, and each room in it, benefits from contrast. This house and its dining room are prime examples. Of course, contrast can come in many different forms, and it need not be obvious or extreme. Color, pattern, material, scale—all are key factors. So are such considerations as period, style, and country of origin.

I love to pair light with dark and old with new. Often in dining rooms, this means an antique table with contemporary chairs or vice versa; it can also be a dark table with light chairs or a light table with dark chairs. Here, I paired the ebonized Regency mahogany table, purchased for one of the couple's earlier New York apartments, with chalky-white Louis XVI–style chairs.

The contrast continues with rustic stained floorboards that make the highly lacquered walls and Empire chandelier shine. In the tradition of the great English country houses, it's all about mixing the old and the new, the refined and the rustic. The floor speaks of history and permanence, with marks of time and life

visible through the stain; the walls, of skilled craftsmanship; the chandelier, of time and so much more.

The painting by Melinda Hackett came from the owners' last New York apartment (see page 205). The canvas is kaleidoscopic, with colors from across the spectrum. This visual complexity, though, is part of what makes it stand out so brilliantly here against the solid walls. Plus, the different reds, so dominant in this painting, feel especially dynamic amid the surrounding browns, blues, and greens.

For me, texture is often the standout in terms of contrast. Imagine any room done entirely in one material. Wouldn't it feel flat? Adding a mix— the linens, the bouclés, the wovens, the wools, the velvets, the leathers—enhances the space and makes it feel distinctive. Here, I paired two materials for the chairs' upholstery—waxed leather seats with Thai silk chairbacks—for visual interest.

In design and decoration, contrast and balance go hand in hand. When they are in harmony, the rooms sing.

PREVIOUS SPREAD, LEFT: Decorative painter Chris Pearson did a masterful job re-creating Albert Hadley's chevron floor. I found the vintage double sconces in Paris and had another pair made for the opposite wall. PREVIOUS SPREAD, RIGHT: In this china cabinet, blue-and-white porcelain from Sotheby's mingles with finds from Pearl River Mart in New York City. OPPOSITE: I love a table setting that elevates the everyday. The bamboo flatware and raffia place mats lighten the formality of this dining room.

ABOVE AND OPPOSITE: The exotic animal prints, photo collage by Peter Beard, and gnarled ceramic garden stool offer an interesting contrast to the library's classical framework and Robert Motherwell print. I often use swing-arm lamps when there is no other way to bring a convenient light source close to the reader.

ABOVE AND OPPOSITE: This game room is a family favorite. The decoration walks the line between formal chic and country casual with a custom Russian-inspired cabinet, rush matting, rattan seating, matchstick shades found online, and Pierre Frey fabric panels lining the walls.

PREVIOUS SPREAD, LEFT: Red and blue are an energizing combination. PREVIOUS SPREAD, RIGHT: I love the play of color and scale of these two seemingly disparate patterns. ABOVE: With the details, it is all about balance. Brass, seagrass, and rattan pop against the blue wool L-shaped sofa. OPPOSITE: The floor of the adjacent butler's pantry picks up the color and pattern play.

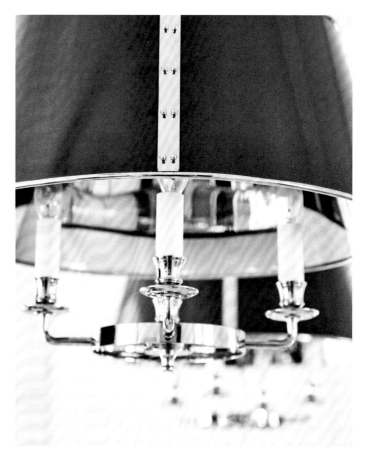

ABOVE: The handmade china and lanterns from Charles Edwards gave us opportunities to carry the Prussian blue from the dining room into the kitchen. OPPOSITE: Architect George Knight created a kitchen that is wonderful for preparing meals as well as a beautiful living space for the family to gather. The island is perfect for snacks and casual meals.

Contrast and scale are the keys to
successfully mixing patterns.
Here, I mixed florals with geometrics
and oversize prints with small
allover ones; they are balanced by
the solid textural white linen of the
upholstered bed frame.

OPPOSITE: Whenever I use a large-scale pattern, like the Lee Jofa fabric that
turns the walls of this principal bedroom into a garden, I calm it down
with a solid. Mixing in more patterns—the Muriel Brandolini fabric lining
the half tester, the D. Porthault bed linens—requires a delicate hand.
The bed by Hickory Chair is inspired by an iconic Syrie Maugham design.

ABOVE: Carefully balanced in terms of scale and color, all the fabrics in the room pull elements from nature. OPPOSITE: I wanted this bedroom to feel like it is in bloom through all four seasons. This photograph by Susanna Howe from Sears-Peyton Gallery, which connects the indoors to the outdoors so vividly, contributes to the effect.

ABOVE AND OPPOSITE: I always look for opportunities to customize a design. In this
principal bathroom, I used what had been a vertical stripe in the Oscar de la Renta paper
as a horizontal border, so that it looks as if the pattern were created just for this room.

ABOVE LEFT: The cotton tape trim on this Roman shade makes this boy's room look tailored and masculine. ABOVE RIGHT: Prussian blue is one connective thread that helps tie the entire house together. OPPOSITE: Upholstering the bed in the same fabric as the walls adds a playful note.

ABOVE AND OPPOSITE: I believe outdoor spaces, like interior rooms, should be
furnished for comfort, function, and beauty. Classic wicker chairs are
comfortable for everything from lounging to dining, making this terrace a
breeze to dress up or down for all the different occasions of family life.

HUNT
COUNTRY
MODERN

This couple purchased their gorgeous hilltop property in Millbrook, New York, for its showstopping setting, not for the existing house, a midcentury-modern ranch. We all foresaw a total rebuild in a few years, so I started the project with a short-term refresh in mind. As the process unfolded, it became increasingly clear how fabulous the house could be. That is when we excitedly launched into a thorough renovation for the long term.

I chose patterns in this house for fun and function, like the happy, overscale fig-leaf design in the sixty-two-foot-long entrance hall and corridor. The pattern works as a take on the old-growth oaks outside and its punchy style introduces tons of character and personality. The same is true of the faux-bois wallpaper for the airy living room, which I opted for because it channeled the space's original, paneled midcentury vibe. Its limed-oak coloring gives the room a twenty-first-century update.

OPPOSITE: I love the play of these Susan Hable botanical prints against the Peter Dunham wallpaper in the entrance hall. Their scale and graphic quality energizes this pass-through between the living room and family room.

I decided to relocate the dining room to the former breakfast room to take advantage of its stunning view of the surrounding landscape. I dressed up its cherry paneled walls in a shade of paint called Rifle Green, a nod to Millbrook's hunt-country heritage. We also designed a new bar, mirroring the back to enhance the view. I reimagined what had been the formal dining room as a family room, removing its crystal chandelier and installing a peacock-blue strié wallpaper and painting the trim to match. I added an oversize L-shaped velvet sofa for weekend lounging and movie nights.

Like all rooms, the principal bedroom was always going to live or die by its furniture plan. I did not want to over-furnish it, so I concentrated on scaling all the elements properly to create warmth and intimacy. I gave the guest room a lift with another variation on the faux-bois motif. In the nursery, I turned over a new leaf pattern, so to speak. This brought the perspective full circle—and made the home complete, stylish, and right for years to come.

PREVIOUS SPREAD AND OPPOSITE: We covered the living room's cherry paneling with a faux-bois wallcovering from Nobilis that feels authentic to this midcentury house. We made sure to follow all the original architectural details, from ceiling beams to built-in bookshelves. The cork tabletop adds more texture into a mix that includes bouclé, metal, and wood.

I believe a house should feel cohesive from the entry hall to the last bedroom wall, so I finish each space to the last square inch.

COMPLETE

Color, pattern, texture, form, scale, light—I see all these elements of design and decoration as much more than visual pleasures. For me, each serves its important purpose. My challenge lies in selecting and combining the specific choices to create livable, comfortable, lasting rooms. I want the homes I design to feel collected and still evolving, but also—and just as important—finished and complete. This is why I work forward from the entrance hall and at the same time backward from the last piece of art in the children's rooms. This parallel process ensures that all the spaces both come into their own and knit together into one organic, cohesive whole.

In this house, the connective tissue is literally built in, with a wonderful circular plan that ties together the living room, dining room, media room, and kitchen. Within this matrix, the living room is intended to deliver everyday comfort—at all hours, in all seasons—for many different functions. The furniture plan lays the foundation. The specific furnishings, fabrics, finishes, and art layer in the function and style.

I try not to start decorating with fabrics. Furniture selection is just as important as the choice of fabrics, rugs, and curtains. But I always tackle the walls first, because when the walls receive such a high degree of care and attention, the rooms and home inevitably feel as though they are part of a whole. I love wallpaper, like the wood-grain pattern here, a play on the room's original paneling. Other favorites include lacquer, panels, Venetian plaster, and specialty decorative finishes. All of which is to say that Sheetrock and paint are not in my lexicon.

Because artwork is integral to the look of a wall, I always consider it from the start. I may begin searching for pieces that are just fun—a print series, perhaps, or some sort of playful work that I can frame in a different way—so the budget can accommodate special pieces over time as they are discovered. Don't feel the most important artwork has to hang over the living room sofa. For this room, we enlarged a simple photograph to go over the L-shaped banquette; it fills the space beautifully and left room in the budget to purchase other more important pieces, like the commissioned oil painting over the turntable. The final details such as custom lampshades, throws, and collected objects make a room feel cohesive and complete.

OPPOSITE: The importance of artwork to making a room feel finished cannot be overstated. Art does not always mean paintings, prints, or pieces that hang flat on perimeter walls. Layering three-dimensional artworks, like this wire sculpture, into a room's interior can energize a negative space.

RIGHT: I love an L-shaped sofa because it really draws people into a room, and it is also very flexible. People can pull up occasional chairs at will to create a conversation hot spot that fits the moment. If you build it, they will come—and make it their own. The photograph by Dustin Ryan commands the wall, and it also ties this space to the exterior view.

ABOVE: An antiqued mirror behind the bar offers another glimpse of the spectacular landscape. Its mottled surface is particularly beautiful at night. OPPOSITE: The trestle dining table of reclaimed barnwood brings in a farm-country feeling, the perfect contrast to the lacquer walls.

OPPOSITE: I wanted to give this room a sense of its place in traditional Millbrook as well as allude to the house's modernist roots. The Roman shade and antelope rug are traditional. The light fixture, in combination with the Arne Jacobsen Egg chair, nods to the house's midcentury heritage.

ABOVE: Pattern play abounds with pillow fabrics, layers of texture, and even repeating forms.

ABOVE: The renovation opened up the original kitchen's three spaces into one gracious, functional room. OPPOSITE: These clients grew up spending lots of time at their kitchen tables, so creating a comfortable breakfast nook was an important consideration. To keep the space from getting too staid, Betty Merken's paintings hang purposefully off-center. The custom laminated fabric on the banquette is virtually indestructible.

PREVIOUS SPREAD: Every element works to bring the principal bedroom's large volume into comfortable scale. Not every piece has to be grand. For example, we chose chaises from Restoration Hardware but reupholstered them in a luxurious wool. ABOVE: A close-up of the scale play. OPPOSITE: A contemporary landscape painting by Michael Abrams continues the room's connection to the outdoors.

ABOVE: In the powder room, the purple sconce shades provide a fun counterbalance to the geometric wood-veneer wallcovering. Hand towels from Julia B. sneak in a note of formality. OPPOSITE: In the home office, the nesting tables and desk chair are vintage finds from Hudson, New York, one of my favorite antiquing haunts.

ABOVE LEFT: This table lamp was one of our fun midcentury online finds. ABOVE RIGHT: Individual reading lights are a thoughtful addition to a twin bedroom. OPPOSITE: Splashes of primary colors and another variation on faux-bois paper add personality to this cheerful guest bedroom.

PREVIOUS SPREAD: We continued the arboreal theme with the nursery's wallpaper, this time in soothing grays and blues. I treated the ceiling as a fifth wall with a high-gloss paint to suggest greater height; the overhead fixture fits the room's large scale beautifully. The layered rugs are perfect for playtime. ABOVE AND OPPOSITE: Old-growth oaks provide an architectural frame for the dining terrace and outdoor seating group.

A HOUSE IN THE CITY

When I met this family, they had recently purchased an Upper East Side brownstone in need of a complete reinvention. Architect Jim Joseph created a beautiful canvas with the structural renovation, opening up the back of the house, restoring the facade, installing a central stair, and seamlessly weaving together old and new. I knew we were in for a lot of fun when we were discussing the design of the bar and the wife requested a disco ball in lieu of a traditional light fixture. Her celebratory spirit elevated every decorating decision I made.

I love an entry hall that both connects to and contrasts with the rest of the rooms. Here, I wanted to establish a serene and stylish welcome. The stone floor was functional enough to stand up to the family dogs and four children on the go; a de Gournay scenic wallpaper gave a subtle nod to nearby Central Park. The kitchen, off the stair landing's other side, took some serious finessing. To make it ultra-usable for today's living, we worked and reworked its layout with

OPPOSITE: The decision to lacquer the paneled hallway was made in concert with choosing white Venetian plaster walls for the living room. Their contrast completely changed the character of both spaces. OVERLEAF: Variety is the spice of life. In this living room, different patterns, colors, textures, periods, and styles work and play together harmoniously.

the architect. Now it flows into a bright, airy family room that unfolds to the garden—city sophistication, connected to the outdoors.

I wanted the living room to become the family's ultimate gathering space for family life. I established different functionalities and conversation groups, all dressed in livable, forgiving fabrics, so this room became the place to be for every occasion, including the children's weekly band practice with their friends. The dining room had to be just as adaptable, a happy space with a Georgian table perfect for everyday meals, frequent dressy dinner parties, and weeknight homework sessions. The bar got a lacquered finish to give the disco ball's dappled light a place to dance.

I wanted to make the most of this principal bedroom's lofty eleven-foot-high ceilings and garden views, so I installed floor-to-ceiling curtains to emphasize the height. I wrapped the walls in a pale blue grass cloth and added a deep, soft rug. For the daughters' shared bedroom, it was a case of "think pink" with a lotus leaf wallpaper that is both graphic and fun. For the younger son's bedroom, I pictured walls, windows, and beds covered in the same fabric, economically managed with a ticking stripe found at Calico Corners. It all comes together in a house that feels happy and fun. And to think it all started with that disco ball.

OPPOSITE: Alex Schuchard's diptych commands the large expanse of wall over the sofa, bringing it back to human scale, and also layers in another take on the room's color palette and patterns drawn from nature. The sofa's cotton velvet brings in the Prussian blue from the hallway. I custom colored one of my favorite fabrics, Bennison's Wheat Flower, with a hint of lavender for the chair.

It is important to mix art mediums within a room, from encaustic oil paintings and photography to paper collage and sculpture. The mix creates excitement and adds balance. Michael Eastman's arresting photograph from Edwynn Houk Gallery provides visual contrast to the room's other artworks in terms of subject, medium, and style.

RIGHT: This room's elements are elegant enough for more formal occasions—the chaise is a favorite gathering spot at cocktail parties—but also welcoming and durable enough that the children feel comfortable using them with their friends. I love to include a desk in the living room. It is a great place to work or take a call, and it can serve as a place to rest a tray during parties. The chair can be pulled into the room as needed.

ABOVE: Like practical jewelry, these brass tables from Liz O'Brien make themselves useful. They are easy to move and so pretty in their simplicity. OPPOSITE: Agnes Barley's collages command this wall with powerful, understated style. Since the sofa's small allover pattern reads almost as a neutral, it adds to the visual interest without distracting.

LEFT: In the entrance hall—a study in black, white, and gray—form and geometry take precedence over color. The grisaille scenic paper from de Gournay references Central Park. The French limestone and wrought iron console table adds to the park and garden motif. The Robert Kelly painting at the base of the stairs introduces a pleasingly sharp modern contrast. OVERLEAF: Lacquered in a custom shade of peacock blue, the custom pieced Gracie paper that covers the dining room walls is both practical and glamorous. John Rosselli made the dining room chairs for us in a perfect scale for the Muriel Brandolini print that upholsters the chairbacks; leather seats in a saturated shade of red as intense as the blue of the walls provide just the right amount of durability for everyday use. The Georgian dining table is a find from Sotheby's.

PAGE 88: In this jewel box of a powder room on the parlor floor, the Hermès paper picks up the palette from the living room.
PAGE 89: The husband purchased the photograph by Melvin Sokolsky for this bar to celebrate the completion of the house and his wife's playful personality, also seen in the disco ball above.
RIGHT: There are many challenges associated with making a kitchen in a New York City brownstone into a functional room for a family of six. Architect Jim Joseph smartly mocked up the island before construction to scale it properly and allow enough space to accommodate the breakfast table.

RIGHT: Bare windows help ensure that the family room off the kitchen feels seamlessly connected to the garden. The scale of the wallpaper pattern is so large, it almost disappears. The photograph by Carol Bouyoucos adds another layer to the indoor-outdoor motif. Along with the view, the Michael S. Smith print on the lounge chair is the seed for all the pattern and color choices. OVERLEAF: Textured walls and a cozy woven rug help turn this principal bedroom into a serene private retreat. Mounting the curtains at the eleven-foot-high crown emphasizes the lofty ceiling height.

PAGE 96: Children's rooms inevitably need to change as the children grow, so economic practicalities always come into play. I like to pick one element of the room, do it really well, and let it be the star. In the daughters' shared bedroom, the Galbraith & Paul Lotus wallpaper serves that purpose. PAGE 97: Both girls agreed on pink, which I grounded with gray accents. Fun, girly headboards from Ballard Designs help tame the room's scale. RIGHT: In one son's bedroom, a Calico Corners striped fabric allowed us to make the same design point of letting one element take the lead. The airplane prints play into the same spirit.

NEW COUNTRY CLASSIC

I trust my instincts, but I always come prepared. I arrived at the initial meeting for this eighteenth-century farmhouse in Millbrook, New York, with the idea of lacquering the double-parlor living room in aubergine, a color I pulled out of the Colefax and Fowler rose-printed chintz I planned to use on the living room chairs. I had a backup plan (and a backup for that plan) in case the deep color and lacquered finish were a bridge too far. To my delight, this couple was all in, so I knew from the get-go that they would be up for taking creative risks.

After moving out of Manhattan, the clients wanted a true country house, not a city house transplanted to the country. Their eighteenth-century, Federal-style house had plenty of history and character, as well as the eccentric floor plan typical of a house that has grown over centuries. We wanted to respect the past, but create living spaces that would be comfortable, inviting, and family-centric. Many of their pieces, antique and otherwise, had come with the house, including lots of upholstery that I re-covered and incorporated throughout as building blocks.

OPPOSITE: This double-height portico is one of the dramatic elements of the original house. With wonderful vintage wicker pieces collected over time, a lantern, and potted ferns, this comfortable porch is used often by the family, both day and night.

I used the entry hall to establish the air of relaxed refinement that felt just right for the family and the house. This space opens to the aubergine-lacquered living room, and to balance the intensity I wove in contrasting shades of green, blue, and white that, like tendrils, reach into the details elsewhere. Two fabulous inherited family pieces—a Georgian table and a Queen Anne-style cabinet—layer the dining room with personal history. I gave the pine-paneled library, a 1950s addition languishing under too many coats of stain, the lacquer treatment too, this time in Prussian blue. Then I bumped up the lighting and added lots of down-filled upholstery to draw people in. As for the cherry red that becomes such an integral part of the color story, I first introduced it in the pass-through off the butler's pantry and kitchen that we turned into a combined sitting room and play space. The red reappears in an eighteenth-century documentary wallpaper in the powder room.

I continued the transformation upstairs, converting the landing into another comfy spot for the children to read or play. Throughout the process, the wife and I would hold our decorating meetings upstairs as the rooms downstairs gradually took shape, light streaming in and views of the countryside from every window. But I will never forget our beginning: that aubergine-lacquered living room, the risk that was so worth taking.

OPPOSITE: Staining and oiling the entry's antique pine boards brought them back to their original glory. My clients acquired the convex Federal mirror with the house. Brown furniture, such as this nineteenth-century console table found at Stair Galleries in Hudson, New York, feels appropriate here. OVERLEAF: An ottoman offers the ultimate in flexibility, providing a handy surface for books or games and extra pull-up seating when necessary.

PAGE 106: With one 1990s show house room, Mario Buatta took the fear out of aubergine lacquer. PAGE 107: Decorative painter Elizabeth Hargraves repaired my client's Venetian mirror by carving and silver-leafing the missing pieces. OPPOSITE: Napoleon III chairs are perfectly scaled to fit in almost everywhere; horsehair stuffing makes the originals incredibly comfortable. ABOVE: Contrast creates harmony when nineteenth-century Regency chairs meet a 1930s Frances Elkins table.

PREVIOUS SPREAD: A masculine tape on the curtains tames the prettiness of the romantic floral fabric. At the baseboard and ceiling, the nailhead tape introduces a hint of aubergine. ABOVE: I love table settings that combine the formal with the everyday. OPPOSITE: The clients inherited this bonnet-top cabinet on stand. We upholstered its back in an Indian block print to bring it into the twenty-first century.

PREVIOUS SPREAD: Organic meets abstract in this paneled library. The neutral antelope rug is a stark contrast to the graphic Sam Francis print over the fireplace. OPPOSITE: I love to use fabrics in unexpected ways, such as framing a Roman shade with a pieced border made from the same Bennison Fabrics print. ABOVE: As Mark Hampton said, every room benefits from a little pop of red.

PREVIOUS SPREAD: The view through the enfilade from the sitting room to the living room captures a snapshot of the house's history. ABOVE: Sometimes an arrangement of leaves gathered from the garden adds just the right note of form and color. OPPOSITE: With an Indian block-printed shade, a swing-arm sconce layers pattern with function.

ABOVE: We emphasized the old-fashioned elements of this powder room by painting the existing trim a deep brown and adding a historic Braquenié floral and bird–printed paper. OPPOSITE: One of the few architectural renovations involved adding the window seat on the upper stair landing between the children's bedrooms. The stenciled grass cloth wallcovering connects the two levels.

LOCAL COLOR

The blessing part of seeing how to make a house more livable is obvious. The curse part? Breaking the news to a Washington, D.C.–based couple that the way to create their personal winter paradise was to remove the pool from the backyard of their newly purchased Florida townhouse. Drastic, I know. But to step out the back door was to practically trip into the pool. My vision was a coral-paved entertaining terrace. Getting the couple to yes was easy once we found an Italian fountain on one of our many shopping jaunts along Dixie Highway in West Palm Beach.

Removing the pool was one of two major gestures I used to brighten up this home and transform it into its best possible self. The other was replacing the dark cherry floors with pickled ash to establish a seamless indoor-outdoor connection. On a more subtle note, architect Kiko Sanchez and I introduced continuous wainscoting in the entry hall and up the stairs to establish a defining baseline throughout. Then I chose the different wall treatments and wallpapers carefully for scale, palette, and personality, knowing they would bring each space into sharper focus.

OPPOSITE: Replacing the house's original dark floors with pickled white ash instantly brightened the space. Adding a wainscot with a pieced Gracie wallpaper above gave the entrance hall architectural presence. An antique Venetian mirror and vintage rattan bench, finds from a Dixie Highway shopping trip, make a statement about this client's desire to live with history and tradition in a modern way.

This couple felt very strongly about using antiques to ground the rooms in history. The wife and I began with some serious local treasure hunting. Early on, we turned up a cache of fabulous pieces that set our direction: the Georgian mirror over the fireplace, the living room's Victorian bamboo cabinet for storing shells, many hard-to-find pieces of Dodie Thayer china to fill out her existing collection, and more.

With a ceiling peaking at eighteen feet, the dining room cried out for visual interest at eye level to make everyone feel cozier and more comfortable. Thinking about the indoor-outdoor connection, I opted for a lacquer-and-lattice wall treatment inspired by a memorable Parish-Hadley room. The library was the natural spot for a home office. The kitchen vista into the palm trees inspired the palette of soft greens, browns, and blues that I wove through the ground-floor spaces and beyond in different intensities. In the principal bedroom, I made sure that every choice accomplished at least three goals: taming the volume, building comfort, and instilling peace and happiness.

As I walked the tightrope between traditional and contemporary to find just the right balance, we made sure to include local references, from the loggerhead turtle wallpaper to shells and handwoven baskets we found in the old-school souvenir shops that still line Dixie Highway. As for the pool? On the sunny terrace, surrounded by tropical foliage and the peaceful sound of the fountain, no one misses it.

OPPOSITE: When a vaulted ceiling peaks at almost eighteen feet, light at different levels—overhead, eye level, and reading—does more than add function. It helps to tame the scale and create comfort. The height also calls for some decorative drama, which the George III mirror over the fireplace supplies in spades.

ABOVE: With the help of architect Kiko Sanchez, we introduced considered architectural details throughout that added charm and brought the spaces into focus. The Victorian bamboo cabinet of natural curiosities and the pelican painting matted in a mollusk-shell frame speak to the Florida coast. OPPOSITE: Custom Fromental panels add verticality and a modern note; the white-lacquer frames walk the line between traditional and contemporary.

INDIA HICKS ISLAND STYLE
VERANDA THE ART OF OUTDOOR LIVING LISA NEWSOM

ABOVE: Ceramic lamps from Christopher Spitzmiller with turquoise lacquered paper shades give this Regency sideboard a twenty-first-century update.
RIGHT: This dining room had so much wall to tackle, it needed a major decorative solution. The lacquered and latticed walls nod to the outdoors. The curtains are a classic Brunschwig & Fils floral. The combination is old-school yet playful.

A passion for collecting beautiful things gives a home so much personality. Displaying the individual pieces together in just the right setting makes the entire collection shine.

OPPOSITE: While working on the house, the client and I searched for additions to her collection of Dodie Thayer china, amassed over the years. One day, we hit the jackpot with a rare soup tureen and a cache of teacups and saucers. With its complementary painted interior, this bleached-mahogany cabinet gives the collection a perfect home.

ABOVE: My friend Katie Ridder designed this turtle-motif paper. I loved its Prussian blue color and its depiction of the loggerhead turtles indigenous to this part of Florida. OPPOSITE: People often worry that dark walls will close in a space, but the opposite is true. In this upstairs sitting room, the deep brown walls recede, letting the furniture and artwork shine.

PREVIOUS SPREAD, LEFT:
The palm trees, which act
like a canopy in this
tropical paradise, made
window treatments in the
kitchen unnecessary.
PREVIOUS SPREAD, RIGHT:
A Nantucket beach scene
above the sofa in the
family room reminds
these clients of another
seaside place they love.
LEFT: Chartreuse grass
cloth at the back
of the bookcase serves
as a punctuation mark
that highlights the form
and texture of the
items displayed. Rattan
chairs from Bielecky
Brothers bring in an old
Florida vibe.

LEFT: For comfort, we added bed hangings to this custom four-poster bed, which helps fill the large volume in the principal bedroom. The small-scale check balances the large-scale botanical print on the walls. A comfortable seating group in front of the window offers a perfect spot for reading.

OPPOSITE AND ABOVE: The terrace, formerly paved in red brick, featured a small pool too close to the house. By removing the pool and replacing the brick with creamy coral stone, we transformed the experience of this house. With an elegant rattan seating area, this outdoor room is now so inviting and livable that no one misses the pool.

THE
DECORATIVE
THREAD

Whenever I get the plans for a house from the architect, I start thinking immediately about how to make the rooms work. My mind goes directly to the walls. I always want to make them an active part of each space, so I consider furniture placement and finishing together. I like to avoid arranging the seating around a fireplace. For instance, in this house in Darien, Connecticut, I decided to pull the seating out to the perimeter to avoid a center mass of legs and corners—no tripping, please. And since one of my personal trade rules is to make the most of every available inch, I designed banquettes for the living and dining rooms to maximize options for family living, playing, and entertaining. The one in the living room is great for the children to bounce on even when the grown-ups are having cocktails. The one in the dining room creates a place for an extra dinner table, a spot for drinks before or dessert after a meal, and another cozy place for the children to play. After all, why not highlight the fun in function?

OPPOSITE: The striped rug in the entrance hall picks up the rhythm of the stair balusters and balances a favorite Quadrille pattern that covers the Napoleon III–style settee. OVERLEAF: This nineteenth-century spoon-back chair fits just about anywhere. The L-shaped banquette is just as comfy for adults as it is for the family's children, who play on it all the time. We repeated the geometry of the contemporary bone-inlaid mirror in the contrast trim of the Roman shades.

In my view of decorating—and, happily, in this family's too—very fun and very pretty are meant for each other. This can lead to some delightful surprises. Most often, one sees a scenic paper in an entrance hall, dining room, or powder room, but it could be considered a stretch for the living room. This couple was game. The scenic paper I chose provided all the cues for what I like to call the decorative thread, which can be a color or a pattern that appears and reappears throughout a house. Here, the pale purple roses from the paper bloom fully in the dining room's aubergine-lacquered walls. The tiniest dot of Prussian blue in a bird tail emerges in the artwork and lamps, then marches through the doorway onto the lacquered walls of the library, which doubles as a home office. For contrast, bursts of red create a chain reaction from the vestibule to the breakfast room, wind around to the butler's pantry, and then spill into the kitchen and the family room.

And who doesn't covet a bedroom nested into the treetops? Since this couple's bedroom looks directly onto leafy branches, I covered its walls with a tree-of-life paper that brings the outside in. One more flight up, I made a hideaway playroom for the children under the eaves. Fun and function sit side by side here and throughout the house.

OPPOSITE: I made sure to draw visual connections between the palettes of the living room and the library. The mossy-green velvet sofa speaks to the Holland & Sherry wool covering the lounge chair. The Prussian blue ceramic table lamp by Christopher Spitzmiller calls out to the lacquered wall panels. Leora Armstrong's painting next to the lamp also marries the two spaces through color.

RIGHT: In the library, the curtains in a Bennison Fabrics floral bring the view inside. The painting by Robert Kelly introduces a bold, abstract note into the mix of more traditional shapes and patterns.

ABOVE: I like to provide a place for movement in the dining room. Here, the banquette by the window is a place for guests to have cocktails before dinner or sit for dessert with a plate on the lap.
OPPOSITE: The dark aubergine walls highlight the shape of the matte-white ceramic lamps. The antique table and sideboard are in lively conversation with the chalky-white klismos chairs.

RIGHT: Throughout this house, pops of red enliven the blues and greens. In this breakfast room, the red in the Lee Jofa floral print and the lantern from the Urban Electric Co. over the table give all the blue and white an extra shot of energy.

ABOVE: Use what you own: silver pitchers at breakfast, pretty tableware, and placemats elevate the everyday. OPPOSITE: The red lacquer and brass accents dress up this small but functional butler's pantry. OVERLEAF: For ultimate functionality, this family kitchen includes built-in silver, linen, and flatware storage and easy-to-clean laminated fabrics.

Mixing different textiles keeps an otherwise summery room from feeling too seasonal. So many great fabrics do not scream winter or summer. Try combining florals with wool and chenille. A beautiful linen chintz feels cool, but the colors can work year-round, especially if you add a colorful cashmere throw for instant warmth.

OPPOSITE: Furnished for comfort, this multifunctional family room unfolds off the kitchen, a perfect gathering spot for adults and children. The custom coffee table, covered in a red grass cloth, serves as a punctuation mark for the creamy palette.

RIGHT: Though large in scale, the eighteenth-century-style tree-of-life pattern enveloping the walls brings a sense of serenity. Paintings by Isabel Bigelow add an abstract note. OVERLEAF, LEFT: In the upstairs playroom, geometry creates harmony: the medallions of the Sanderson wallpaper repeat the shape of the Noguchi lantern and contrast with the striped rug. OVERLEAF, RIGHT: For the bedroom of this little boy who loves cars, we began with the prints and layered in more fun color with the turquoise and lime-green accents.

THE LIGHT TOUCH

People who grew up in Florida, as I did, and now live where it snows, still crave the homes of our childhood: light, bright, and seamlessly connected to the outdoors. So when this husband, a fellow Floridian, explained that he and his wife wanted to open up their Georgian Revival–style house in Greenwich, Connecticut, to the light and the landscape, I understood their vision immediately. The house dates to the early 2000s, and I was fortunate to work with Louise Brooks, its original architect, on the renovation's major strokes: adding huge windows and French doors, bleaching the floors, moving the pool closer to the house, and building a loggia on the pool's original site.

My approach to decorating here was a search for common ground. The husband loves contemporary and midcentury modern. The wife adores color and pattern. I wanted to honor both and compromise neither. The two had already assembled a wonderful collection of midcentury pieces, which I helped develop into a broader mix throughout. To soften the furniture's strict lines, I used timeless textures and patterns. To hold the ornamentation in check, I kept a disciplined eye on form, pattern, and color.

OPPOSITE: The simplicity of the white grass cloth we used in this double-height entry hall brings the geometry of curves and lines to the fore. In the midst of all the lightness and brightness, the citrine-lacquered tabletop introduces a brilliant pop of color that energizes the entire space.

ABOVE: The custom peacock-blue top of the Roman Thomas coffee table is a modern take on parchment, a beloved midcentury material. OPPOSITE: From the wood-veneer wallcovering to the contemporary upholstered seating and the client's midcentury pieces, including the rosewood chair by Gio Ponti in the foreground and the klismos-style bench by T. H. Robsjohn-Gibbings by the fireplace, this room marries form with function.

In the double-height entrance hall, I took a less-is-more approach to emphasize the "aha!" moment of the soaring volume. The living room and adjacent music room, though, needed more attention. With a few architectural tweaks to the living room (replacing the mantel, adding French doors, widening the door casings) and a gut renovation of the adjacent paneled music room, we completely recast these two spaces into much fresher, sunnier connected environments. Since the dining room serves as the main downstairs artery, it needed energy and contrast. The solution? A traditional scenic paper with a seriously modern twist on palette and pattern.

The kitchen evolved. First, we planned to paint the cabinets and replace the countertops. Ultimately, to deal with a huge, chimneylike stone backsplash, we took the space down to the studs and added a limed-oak island and an easily maintained pleather banquette, turning the room into a perfect everyday gathering spot open to the family room.

Upstairs, the story is a tale of scale, continuity, and connection. I tinkered with scale throughout. In the principal bedroom, I used patterns and furnishings, including a four-poster bed that brings volume to the room's center. In the children's hideaways, we lowered the vaulted ceilings to make the spaces more embracing.

With these changes and the views of the Long Island Sound from almost every room, this house is now light-filled, bright, and comfortable for busy family life.

PREVIOUS SPREAD, LEFT: The desk at the window expands the living room's usable space. These Robert Mangold prints are at home next to the Harry Bertoia sculpture. PREVIOUS SPREAD, RIGHT: I am always on the hunt for containers that look just as beautiful empty as full. OPPOSITE: The pale woods and citrus tones help the living room communicate with the entrance hall.

ABOVE: We replaced the top of this nineteenth-century tric trac table with bright yellow leather, in keeping with the room's spirit. The wall sculptures by Andrew Zimmerman are from Sears-Peyton Gallery.
OPPOSITE: A thread of pattern ties the living room and music room together. Remounted in a custom maple frame, this abstract pastel from a vintage shop in Hudson, New York, reveals its true beauty.

When working with pattern, it's important to vary the scale, even if the prints are connected by color. Proportion is everything. Incorporating natural materials, such as wicker, bamboo, or rattan, instantly puts a room at ease.

RIGHT: When I saw this antique dhurrie, it was love at first sight. We added a bright blue trim to the matchstick shades made in India. The print by Mel Bochner was a serendipitous discovery in one of my favorite stores, Avery & Dash Collections, in Stamford, Connecticut.

ABOVE AND RIGHT: The custom Fromental mural, with its bright chartreuse ground, makes this dining room a happy place to be for all purposes. Raffia, cane, and wicker details keep the formality in check. The light fixture from Gerald Bland in New York City adds a sculptural note.

OPPOSITE: Comparatively simple curtains let the beauty of the paper sing. The cane chairbacks introduce a note of refined rusticity and act almost like a scrim in changing the view without obscuring it. ABOVE, CLOCKWISE FROM TOP LEFT: Details contribute to an elegant garden feel, from the white sunburst light fixture by Alexander von Eikh to the grassy print on the custom lampshades, floral raffia rug, and hand-painted butterflies.

PREVIOUS SPREAD: Adding planked wood ceilings and the limed-oak island brought warmth to an otherwise all-white kitchen. These simple but sculptural glass pendants from the Urban Electric Co. work in tandem with the more contemporary wrought-iron chandelier over the breakfast table; notes of brass connect the dots. We added a built-in banquette for both functionality and a punch of color through its bright-blue vinyl upholstery. RIGHT: In the family room, which lives directly off the kitchen and breakfast area, carefully balanced layers of pattern prove to be playful and restful against the leafy backdrop of the oversize windows. The acrylic painting by Agnes Barley between the windows and the oils by Isabel Bigelow above the sofa contribute to the happy mood.

ABOVE: When I am working out color combinations, I look across the color wheel to find natural complements, such as yellow and blue. The contrast instantly provides energy, while the neutral geometric rug imparts a sense of calm. OPPOSITE: Found at auction, the vintage Pierre Jeanneret table and chairs show the marks of time.

Connecting each interior vista to the next and those beyond creates a visual continuity that instills comfort and makes the house feel finished.

CONNECTION

I want my clients to really live in and love every part of their homes. It is so important to create visual connections that tie the entire interior together. I never focus just on what a single room looks like. I always have the next space, and those beyond it, in my mind's eye. I never want just one color or a single element to be jarring in any way or stand out as a "wow" moment. For the eye to relax, it needs to see a color more than once, even if it is just the welt on a pillow, the button on a chair, or a piece of art.

There are times when it makes sense to tie adjoining rooms to one another quite subtly and times when I want to make the link between two spaces more obvious. For this sitting area off the principal bedroom, I decided to establish a continuity of pattern and color to weave the two rooms together. To make this area feel cohesive with the rest of the house, I continued the blue from downstairs as well as the block prints that add so much charm and freshness. To give the vestibule its own character (but one related to the principal bedroom), I played with the scale of the patterns and the tones of the blues. In my view, connecting rooms in this way is decorating that is practical, purposeful, and peaceful.

OPPOSITE: A custom lantern ties the vestibule to the principal bedroom with a smaller-scale version of the Indian block-print pattern used for the bedroom's curtains and valance. Both fabrics were custom colored and printed in India. The lantern's contrast banding picks up on the same shade of ultramarine in the window fabric's border. OVERLEAF: The Syrian mirror enhances the bedroom's eclectic notes. The client's japanned étagère was the inspiration for introducing other dark values, including the wrought-iron bed, fireplace surround, papier-mâché birds by Mark Gagnon, and artwork by Shelley Reed.

OPPOSITE: Matte-white details, including the ceramic garden stool, the plaster sconces, and the limestone mantel, serve as a foil for the brown wood and iron elements. ABOVE, CLOCKWISE FROM TOP LEFT: Each detail in this suite of rooms plays a different variation of the decorative theme, whether on the curtains, wall, or throw pillows—or on a desk chair that proves yet again that nothing illuminates a space like a Fortuny fabric.

In searching for artwork for a particular room, many factors must be considered: composition, color, and medium all play a role, but perhaps the most important and often neglected element is scale. The artwork needs to stand up to the size of the wall, the height of the ceiling, and the other decorative elements.

ABOVE: So many of this room's shapes and patterns pick up on decorative motifs used elsewhere in the house without repeating them verbatim. I always like to throw in one oddball pattern in every room; in this case, the ikat pillow picks up the color palette in an unexpected way. OPPOSITE: D. Porthault bed linens and simple cotton coverlets feel like a match made in heaven here. The mix of patterns is fun, young, and playful.

ABOVE: This classic Hinson splatter wallpaper pattern brings life to any space. OPPOSITE: Brilliant reds, turquoise blues, and yellows offer a fun, different take on the classic boy's room palette. Crate & Barrel bunk beds are perfect for sleepovers; cutting down standard twin sheets and coverlets makes the tuck-in easier. OVERLEAF: Working with original architect Louise Brooks, we added this loggia and fireplace and filled it with comfortable seating to make it a destination all year.

LIVING
HISTORY

This family had acquired their apartment in one of James Carpenter's circa-1927 buildings long after successive modifications had stripped away much of the original detail. With the architect Tom Felton, we gave the living spaces the top-to-bottom transformation that brought them up to date and restored many of their former glories. We added arched openings off the foyer, an original detail that had been lost. We restored or replaced moldings that had been removed or modified over time. We totally gutted and re-created the kitchen with many charming details like the steel casement windows that would be true to the 1920s. And we reimagined the former butler's pantry with new cabinetry that incorporated glass panes from the apartment's original windows, all of which we had to replace. Carpenter's elegant, trademark "off-the-foyer" plan had connected each of the principal rooms to a spacious double-height stair hall. This layout was way too gracious to lose, so I made sure all my choices intertwined these spaces visually and cohesively.

OPPOSITE: The stair was one of the few original features of the apartment that had survived intact. Architect Tom Felton and I made careful modifications to the balusters, removing some of the flourishes to make the design feel more current. The chinoiserie light fixture from Charles Edwards complements the scenic wallpaper from Gracie.

I started to balance past and present in the double-height entry hall with a scenic wallpaper that speaks to the past but also feels timely and brings the volume back to earth. I planned the living room to be adaptable, an entertaining space intimate enough for small groups and comfortable for large gatherings. The library became a cozy retreat with a favorite Peter Beard collage. And the dining room became the showstopper, lacquered a delicious candy-apple red with graphic stained floors inspired by a classic marble pattern at the Louvre in Paris that creates a perfect foil for Melinda Hackett's kaleidoscopic painting, that was found quite serendipitiously. Experience has taught me that sometimes a spontaneous find at the end will bring all the elements together. On a visit to Melinda's studio, my client and I were going through all her framed pieces on display when I suddenly spotted a slightly worn rolled-up canvas in a back storeroom. I could see from the exposed corner that it incorporated all the colors of the palette for this apartment, but on steroids. When I installed the painting, it electrified the dining room and energized the first floor.

Upstairs, everything gets quieter and softer. To transform the principal bedroom into a retreat, I used a soothing palette, a half tester over the bed, and a custom-colored Bennison fabric on the walls. In the children's rooms, I maximized the available floor space by using day beds so they could spread out and play.

As top-to-bottom renovations go, this one is transformational. It tells a story of continuity and change. Yet the decoration honors yesterday, today, and tomorrow.

OPPOSITE: Victoria & Son custom made the hall console table specifically to fit this spot; its hand-painted faux-marble top is a whimsical take on natural materials. The twenty-nine-inch-high wainscot we added is perfectly proportioned to make the eleven-foot ceilings soar.

RIGHT: One pair of sconces is a vintage find from the Marché aux Puces in Paris; the second we had made to match. I generally prefer not to mix metals within the same space, but here the different finishes add quite a bit to the room's collected sensibility. Tiger velvet brings an instant sense of elegance to any space— and it actually gets better with age.

ABOVE AND OPPOSITE: Red anemones look brilliant on a marble stool. This custom one-armed chaise offers the perfect extra seating spot for a buffet dinner and is a favorite gathering place during cocktail parties. The curves of the stool offer a pretty contrast to the custom Russian-style cabinet.

ABOVE AND RIGHT: When libraries feel collected and layered, they truly come alive. Favorite art, objects, and travel finds—the Peter Beard collage, vintage brass lion, and tortoise shell—set the tone for this tailored library that nods to the exotic.

Don't be afraid to be bold in the dining room. It's not an everyday space, so color choices can be more dramatic—especially given that they are often viewed at night and by flattering candlelight.

OPPOSITE: These walls are almost edible thanks to Agustin Hurtado, the master painter who applied layers upon layers of lacquer to achieve the same intense color and translucent quality as the candy apples that inspired them. His faux marquetry transforms the floor with another layer of artistry.

OPPOSITE: I believe beautiful rooms should feel livable, not fancy. Introducing one informal, almost rustic, element can make an otherwise formal room feel inviting. Framed by hand-embroidered silk curtains, the bamboo matchstick shades serve that purpose here. ABOVE: Matching the intensity of the walls, Melinda Hackett's painting shifts this essentially traditional room into the twenty-first century.

ABOVE: In this dramatic bar surrounded by faux-tortoise walls, mirrors, crystal, and vintage silver add sparkle by design. OPPOSITE: Lighting at different levels, cabinet glass from the apartment's original windows, and a luminous mesh-paneled lantern combine to give this butler's pantry a soft glow.

ABOVE AND OPPOSITE: Bed-curtains made from a Bennison fabric and a custom pattern on the walls create a heavenly combination of different scales, patterns, and soft palettes in this serene principal bedroom. Adding more curves into the mix of shapes, the Christopher Spitzmiller lamps on the bedside tables supplement the pinpoint glow from reading lights placed conveniently by the headboard.

RIGHT: I am always trying to come up with a fresh palette for boys' rooms, like this combination of orange and blue. The tape trim and nailheads that outline the room's molding lend a masculine but youthful touch. After reframing, the balloon photographs fit the room's lighthearted spirit.

ABOVE: Katie Ridder's Beetlecat wallpaper is an unexpected, playful choice for a boy's bath in the city. Monogrammed Leontine towels with a wave appliqué complete the look. OPPOSITE: Albert Hadley's Fireworks wallpaper adds instant charm everywhere it goes. Framed copies of pages from a beloved book—like these from *The Cat in the Hat*—can be the perfect finishing touches for a child's room.

THE LONG VIEW

I have always dreamed of building a house from the ground up. In the meantime, I had fun renovating and decorating the house in Millbrook my husband shared with his two girls before we were married. We had originally planned to renovate this house after our son was born, but we realized it was never going to give us the view my husband craved. Luckily, we found a fabulous parcel of land in Millbrook, and building the dream house suddenly became a reality. Working with architect Michael Elfenbein, I had the floor plan in mind from the start: a great family kitchen with a wonderful breakfast table connected to a family room via a generous cased opening, a dining room, and my husband's office, all tied into the landscape.

I envisioned our family room as the Millbrook version of my mother's Florida room. The whole scheme started with a Michael Smith chintz in my favorite blues and murky, odd camouflage greens that are so true to my sportsman husband and set the tone for the entire house. With reclaimed beams overhead, silk burlap on the walls, the vintage antlers my husband loves, and antique brown furniture—not my usual go-to, but appropriate here for its sense of history—this room centers our family life.

OPPOSITE: After coveting this American folk art tinsel painting for years, I finally purchased it from my friend and antique dealer Angus Wilkie. It glows in this spot in the stair hall, catching both the morning and afternoon light. Reprinted from nineteenth-century designs, the stairwell's Braquenié fabric adds history and verticality.

Knowing that my palette throughout would lean toward blues and greens, I wanted red for contrast in the entrance hall and a fabric reprinted from nineteenth-century designs, truly timeless since it feels as fresh today as it must have then. The dining room called for a scenic wallpaper—of course—but one more appropriate to our farm-country surroundings than the vines, flowers, and birds I use so often. I love its rustic sepia tones with the formality of the crystal chandelier, lacquered doors, and eighteenth-century chairs, a hand-me-down from my dear friend Chris Spitzmiller.

The kitchen's view into the family room launched the entire floor plan. I can stand at the island and see my son eating breakfast and my husband and stepdaughters reading at the fireplace—each of us doing our thing in separate rooms, but still together.

On the second floor, my son has his tree house–like hideaway in full-on faux bois under the eaves. My stepdaughters' bright, colorful bedrooms on the third floor radiate their joyful energy.

So many things in this house are fun, happy finds discovered with friends and family, purchased at auction, or custom made by some of my favorite craftspeople. They give this house their history—not so much their provenance as our provenance with them, the memory of good times. These memories and so many others bring me joy every day.

OPPOSITE: This Millbrook version of the Florida room of my childhood is the center of our family life. Flanked by vintage antlers, the Black Forest stag above the mirror once belonged to Mario Buatta, and to Michael Taylor before him. The earthy greens and large scale of the chair's Michael Smith fabric contribute to the country feel. OVERLEAF: With two seating groups centered off back-to-back sofas, the floor plan addresses two distinct uses: one for TV and Andrew, our son, playing with his toys; the other for sitting by the fire and entertaining guests at night.

PREVIOUS SPREAD: With all the practicality of a bookcase, antique étagères are a wonderful way to bring furniture to the room's perimeter. This room has two—one William IV; the other Victorian—that ground an arrangement of botanicals topped by a pair of nineteenth-century witches' mirrors from the collection of Mario Buatta. RIGHT: Like a great backdrop, this pastoral scenic paper allows everything else around it to shine, including citrine wool curtains that sing in daylight and glow in candlelight. The Empire chandelier adds sparkle.

232

In a small room, an allover pattern can fool the eye and help the room feel larger by making the walls recede. Here, a garden pattern brings the outside in.

RIGHT: Our daily life starts and ends in the kitchen. To me, it is the epitome of form following function. While I am preparing meals at the island, I can see and talk to my family gathered at the farm table. The sink overlooks the view, and the entire space is filled with natural light from well-placed windows and glass doors to the back terrace and loggia.

Design and decoration can be about so many things. But for me, above all, they are the tools I use to create comfort and a sense of welcome.

COMFORT

Comfort lives in so many aspects of design and decorating. Furniture planning, upholstery, lighting, and the indoor-outdoor connection all factor into it, but architectural flow is key.

To keep the footprint of our house comparatively modest, I wanted a circular plan on the first floor to make the spaces feel expansive and gracious. When we have a party, we can welcome as many as one hundred people easily, not because of the size of the rooms, but because of the way they open to one another and to the landscape.

To be comfortable, a house needs to belong to the whole family and should never look like the decorator just left the room. Here I had to put aside my preference for pretty, and bring in the rustic, so everyone felt at home. Our family room, for example, started with the rough-hewn beams on the ceiling and surrounding the fireplace. The interior decoration followed with the murky greens and bright blues that felt appropriate not just to Millbrook but to our family.

Light is another crucial aspect of comfort. The windows, based on a sill-at-the-floor style prominent in the early 1800s, give the family room brightness and forge a seamless connection to the outdoors. With a pair of chandeliers, picture lights, sconces, and well-placed reading lamps, this room functions beautifully day and night. The curtains add warmth, and the bamboo shades offer a sense of privacy.

Connection is a source of comfort, which brings us back to the flow of a house and why it matters so much. Although we live primarily in our family room, my husband's office is in some ways the heart of the house. Thanks to its proximity, the children can all pop in, sit near his desk, and do homework or play. And its lacquered door, closed as necessary, offers a terrific contrast to all the reclaimed, rough-hewn, and organic elements of the family room.

At the end of the day, when we gather together around our kitchen table to talk, prepare dinner, and eat, we are surrounded by all the people and things we love. This, to me, is the essence of comfort and the meaning of home.

OPPOSITE: This view from the kitchen to the family room is the one that launched the entire floor plan, and it brings me so much comfort. The tole light fixture provides a canopy of warmth over this table, which is used morning, noon, and night.

OPPOSITE: I had this guest bedroom wall fabric custom block-printed in India. ABOVE: This Georgian bowfront chest, though not exactly museum-quality, holds many memories for me. A gift from my grandmother, it is the first piece of antique furniture I ever owned.

PREVIOUS SPREAD: We emphasized the coziness of this charming third-floor bedroom under the eaves by enveloping the room in an eighteenth-century Brunschwig & Fils paper called Bird and Thistle. ABOVE: Favorite details include the vintage bird prints and harmoniously paired D. Porthault linens. OPPOSITE: My friend, the decorative painter Elizabeth Hargraves, gave this antique chair its chalky-white finish, and I had it reupholstered in a favorite silk ikat.

ABOVE: I love grouping family photos together; here, I placed them in a well-traveled bedroom hallway where they are an everyday reminder of our family life. OPPOSITE: My son's bedroom, papered in this navy faux-bois, feels like a tree house full of his favorite things. I found this antique child's chair at Sotheby's. I loved it for its green patent leather seat. I believe that once a child's room is decorated, it is important to let it evolve as they grow with their artwork, toys, and found objects.

RIGHT: Dutchess, our yellow Lab, loves to nap in the sun in the mudroom. This side entrance is a welcome spot full of great storage. The wrought-iron bridle hooks are sturdy enough to handle all of the coats and hats essential to country life. Here and throughout much of the ground floor, reclaimed ceiling beams add character and a great sense of history.

ABOVE AND OPPOSITE: The view was the reason we bought the property, and when planning the house, I made sure we included an expansive loggia and terraces. With a mix of wicker, wrought iron, and teak, the furnishings are just as layered as the house's interiors. In the summer, we live in these outdoor rooms.

ACKNOWLEDGMENTS

To my family, Andrew, Lachlan, Kyla, and Andrew Spence. Thank you for inspiring me to do my best every day and for living the joyful life for which I had the great pleasure of creating our very own well-loved house. It would not be a home without the four of you (oh, and Dutchess...five.)

To my other family, Chris Spitzmiller and Anthony Bellomo. I count your friendship as one of my greatest blessings. Thank you for being the most reliable, fun-loving, kind, generous friends one could ask for. And to Chris for his beautiful foreword and for taking the plunge into the publishing world. You forged a clear path and a confidence in me that I, too, could make something very special.

To Rizzoli, for your faith in me and my process in creating this book. A special thanks to Kathleen Jayes for her keen editing eye and all the care, time, and attention she has given *The Well-Loved House.* To Jill Cohen and her trusted associate Melissa Powell, your enthusiasm and advice in creating this book was unparalleled. I knew from the get-go I was in the best of hands, and for that you will always be appreciated. To Doug Turshen and Steve Turner, for your spectacular design. As they say, "Stand back and watch the masters work." And that you did—thank you.

To my clients, for letting me into their houses and their lives and for trusting me to design homes they will cherish for a very long time. Thank you for letting me push you (and sometimes myself) out of our comfort zones to create something truly special for each of you. I could do nothing without your kindness, loyalty, and—most important—friendship.

To the master lensmen who do everything to make my work look good: Eric Piasecki, Francesco Lagnese, Read McKendree, Max Kim-Bee, George Ross, and Thomas Loof. I know it takes a certain temperament to be a photographer, and having six people hanging over your laptop watching a candlestick move three inches to the left without snapping like a twig is a miracle unto itself. Thank you for your patience and genius at what you do.

To the incredible stylists Carolyn Englefield, Senga Mortimer, Olga Naiman, Dayle Wood, and Heather Chadduck, who make what I do come to life. Not once have I walked away from a shoot without learning something from your brilliant, creative, beautiful process.

To the editors who have been so supportive of my work—namely Newell Turner, who saw something early on in what I was doing and gave me confidence that I was on the right path. Thank you to Sophie Donelson, Whitney Robinson, Margot Shaw, Steele Marcoux, DJ Carey, Clint Smith, and Dara Caponigro.

To my incredible staff, past and present. You make coming to work each day a joy, and your talents and perseverance in getting a job done cannot be underestimated. Alex Wilson, Michael Capuano, Richard Monreal, Millie Waller, Alessandra Marinello, Lena Kerno, Georgie Tipper, Katie Salmon, Katherine Nedelkoff, and Lucy Doswell—thank you for helping make this book a reality. To say I couldn't have done it without you would be putting it mildly, and for that please accept my deepest thanks.

CREDITS

All photography by Thomas Loof except for the following:

Max Kim-Bee: 6, 75-99, 125-143

Francesco Lagnese: 101, 104-105, 106, 118-123

Read McKendree: 145-157, 165

George Ross Photographs: 158-164

Eric Piasecki: 203-223

Peter Beard, "Giraffes in the Mirage on the Taru Desert, Kenya" © 2021 The Estate of Peter Beard / Licensed by Artists Rights Society (ARS), New York: 26, 211

Robert Motherwell, "Pope's Abyss" © 2021 Dedalus Foundation, Inc. / Artists Rights Society (ARS), NY: 27

First published in the United States of America in 2021 by Rizzoli International Publications, Inc.
300 Park Avenue South
New York, NY 10010
www.rizzoliusa.com

Copyright © 2021 Ashley Whittaker
Foreword: Christopher Spitzmiller

Publisher: Charles Miers
Senior Editor: Kathleen Jayes
Design: Doug Turshen with Steve Turner
Production Manager: Alyn Evans
Managing Editor: Lynn Scrabis

Developed in collaboration with Jill Cohen Associates, LLC.

Printed in China

2022 2023 2024 2025 / 10 9 8 7 6 5 4 3

ISBN: 978-0-8478-6952-7
Library of Congress Control Number: 2021937541

Visit us online:
Facebook.com/RizzoliNewYork
Twitter: @Rizzoli_Books
Instagram.com/RizzoliBooks
Pinterest.com/RizzoliBooks
Youtube.com/user/RizzoliNY
Issuu.com/Rizzoli

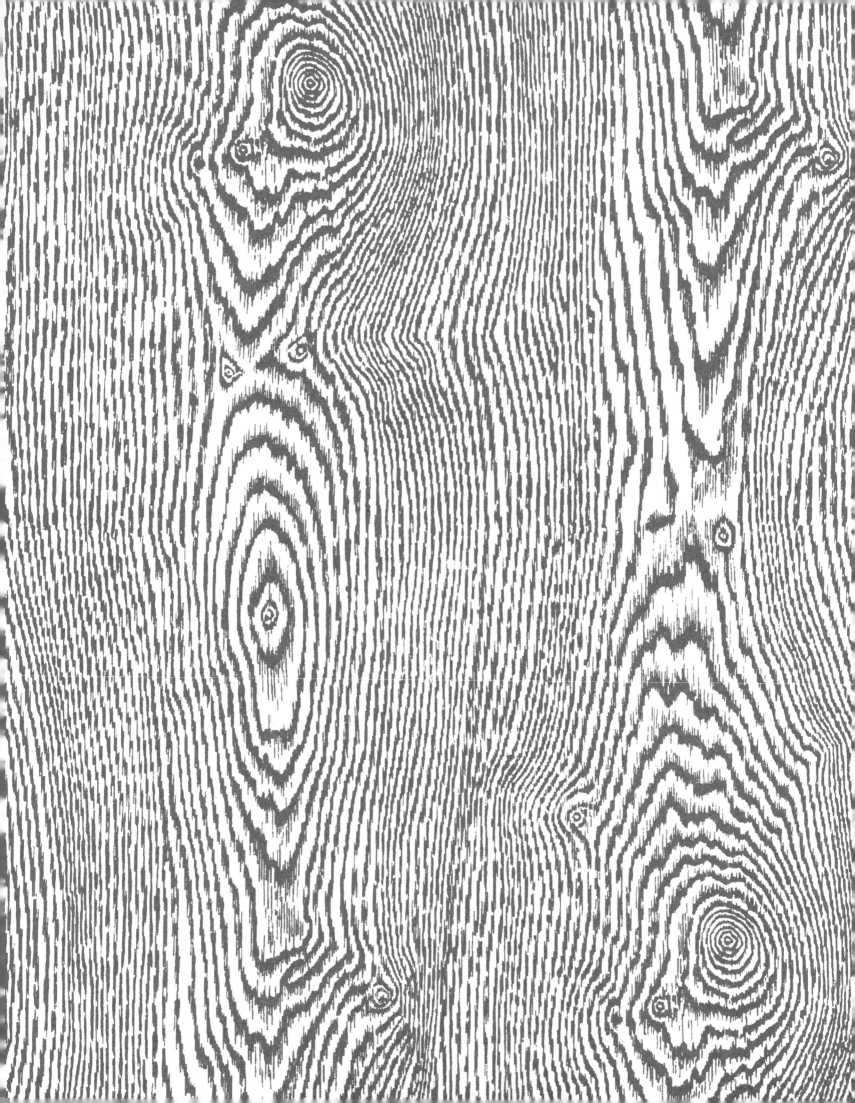